A History of the United Nations Security Council and How to Fix It

A History of the United Nations Security Council and How to Fix It

Intergovernmental Organizations Have Never Been This Exciting

Jason Cappelloni, Veer Juneja, and Anthony Reynolds

Copyright © 2021 Saurav Kumar

All rights reserved.

ISBN-13: 9798495411142

Dedicated to Saurav Kumar

Table of Contents

Introduction – 9

The United States of America – 22

The People's Republic of China – 28

The Russian Federation – 38

The United Kingdom - 44

The French Republic - 52

Non-Permanent Member Countries - 58

Conclusion – 67

References - 75

Introduction

Following the second World War, there was a large increase in the desire for international institutions among countries that held economic and military power in order to prevent future conflicts. The United Nations Security Council was created with the purpose of creating and enforcing intergovernmental cooperation over issues dealing with international security. This council was made to determine how the international community should react to and manage conflicts around the world. However, since the founding of the United Nations Security Council in 1946 there have not been any major changes to it. The lack of change does not stem from a lack of problems, but rather an abundance of problems many of which are preventing the council from being fixed. The United Nations Security Council has not been a complete failure but it has had many instances of large-scale failures that are indicative of systemic issues with the council's ability to actually protect international security. This book seeks to explain the history of the United Nations Security Council, why it has in many cases failed to promote security, and what can be done to solve the issues that have plagued both the council's efficacy and efficiency. Before understanding these problems and proposed solutions, however, one must first understand how the council works.

Membership

While it originally consisted of eleven members, the current United Nations Security Council is composed of fifteen different member countries. These countries are split into two categories: permanent and non-permanent members. There are five permanent members of the council who have retained their position since the founding of the council in 1946. These countries are Russia, China, France, the United Kingdom, and the United States. Since they were the countries that had the most military, political, and economic influence in the world order after the second world war, they essentially made the rules of the council, so it makes sense that they ended up with the most permanent power.

These members, referred to in much of the literature about the council as the P5, are endowed with both permanence on the council and the all-important veto power which allows any one of these countries to stop the council from taking action on an issue. This power is the largest advantage of being a permanent member and by far the most controversial aspect of the council. In addition to the five permanent members, there are also 10 non-permanent members who are elected every other year for a two-year term with a rule in place to ensure that a non-permanent member cannot serve two consecutive terms. These elections happen not through the council itself but rather through the United Nations General Assembly. These elections happen via a secret ballot, which allows members of the assembly to vote without having to explain why, and in order for a country to gain a seat on the council, they need a two-thirds majority. This requirement causes most of the countries who win a non-permanent seat on the council to be countries that hold relatively uncontroversial opinions and are popular with the vast majority of countries that are in the United Nations.

In order to determine who is on the ballot during these elections, two criteria are used. First, whether or not the country could potentially help maintain peace and security. Second is the geographic distribution of countries with Africa having three seats, Latin America and the Caribbean having two, Eastern Europe having one, the Asia-Pacific having two, and a final group called the Western European and Others Group having two. Because these groupings largely exclude Middle Eastern countries, there is an informal agreement that created what is known as the Arab swing seat that alternates between taking up one of the Asia-Pacific or African seats. These non-permanent seats are highly coveted by many different countries, but they do not offer nearly the same power as permanent members have in the security council's proceedings.

However, they still do have some influence as can be seen most clearly through the position of president of the security council. The presidency rotates every month in alphabetical order and is occupied by both permanent and non-permanent countries. The power of the presidency can be viewed as similar to the powers possessed by the Speaker of the House in the United States House of Representatives but to a much lesser extent. Essentially, the president has power over setting the agenda and is supposed to resolve conflicts between countries in order to ensure that the council can protect international security effectively.

The power to set the agenda is by far the most influential aspect of the presidency, but the fact that it only lasts thirty days means that aside from delaying action by a month this power does not change much. This is exacerbated by the fact that any permanent member could veto something which means regardless of the order of the agenda they can still prevent anything they do not like from happening. The responsibility to mediate conflicts between other member countries does not actually give the president the leverage to do it, so aside from denouncing countries that are stopping progress the president cannot force uncooperative countries to work together. Both of these powers, while making the president more influential than they normally would be, ultimately fail to give any substantive influence to most non-permanent countries.

Powers of the United Nations Security Council

The final aspect of the United Nations Security Council that is important to understand is what they actually have the power to do in the rare circumstances where a resolution is passed without being vetoed. There are three main categories of ways in which the council manages threats to international security: declarations, sanctions, and military force.

It is important to note that very frequently in situations where the security council fails to act on something, individual member countries act on it anyway. While the united front of the United Nations is certainly more effective, it is oftentimes far more efficient and practical for countries to take security concerns into their own hands. So, while the tools discussed in this chapter have been used in various situations, it is important to understand that in the vast majority of situations countries act on their own.

The first step the United Nations Security Council takes to resolve conflict is peaceful negotiations and declarations. This generally comes in the form of the United Nations Security Council simply making a resolution known to the public without offering an enforcement mechanism. Usually, it is the threat of future measures that deter countries from ignoring these resolutions. One such example is United Nations Security Council Resolution 2532 which declares a global ceasefire in all instances except against groups recognized as terrorists by the security council. If a country does not listen to these declarations, one of the other two forms of conflict management are usually used.

The second way in which the council can manage conflicts is through sanctions. While initially sanctions were rarely used by the security council, they are now the primary tool the council utilizes. It is important to note that due to human rights concerns the vast majority of sanctions the security council imposes are usually on comprehensive lists of individuals instead of individual countries. One example of this is United Nations Security Council Resolution 1373 which came after the September 11th attacks on the United States sanctioned members of Al-Qaeda as well as the Taliban. It is important to note that when individuals or countries are sanctioned by the security council all members of the United Nations, not just members of the security council, are obligated to sanction them.

The final measure that the security council takes to manage conflict is military intervention, which is also by far the rarest for fairly obvious reasons. One of the only examples of military force ever being authorized is United Nations Security Council Resolution 1973, which authorized military intervention into the first Libyan Civil War. This resulted in the deployment of fighter jets, submarines, and troops into Libya and was ultimately successfully defending Benghazi. While all three methods of conflict have historically been effective at resolving issues, the veto power and unrepresentative nature of the council means these measures do not get used nearly as much as they are needed. While in theory the United Nations Security Council could be effective, in practice it has historically failed to promote peace. This book will analyze each permanent member country, the history of their involvement on the Security Council, and why the Security Council is failing.

The United States of America

The United States has been extremely important to the founding and history of the United Nations Security Council. As the country with the most military and economic strength for most of the past century, they were one of the most influential countries in the postwar world order and one of the countries leading the creation of both the United Nations and the United Nations Security Council.

However, when helping to found the council the United States failed to anticipate the extent to which they would be competing with China and the Soviet Union in the future. While the Republic of

China was a U.S. ally during the creation of the Security Council, in 1971 they were replaced in the United Nations and the United Nations Security Council by the People's Republic of China which has historically been in conflict with the United States and sided with the Soviet Union during the Cold War. Due to both the United States and the Soviet Union having interests in most global conflicts and having the ability to stop any Security Council action with the veto, the Security Council largely was unable to take any substantive action until the end of the Cold War.

After the Cold War, the United States has used its economic and military strength to have greater control over the Security Council than any other permanent member. One example of this came after Iraq invaded Kuwait in 1990, which was responded to with United States Security Council Resolution 678. This resolution gave Iraq a hard deadline to withdraw from Kuwait and after the deadline it allowed members of the Security Council to use any means necessary to remove Iraq. These policies aligned directly with U.S. foreign policy interests in the region and showcases to what extent the U.S. could take control of the Security Council for their own objectives.

This can be seen through the incentives the United States gave to countries that voted with them and the backlash countries that voted against the resolution received. The United States along with

Saudi Arabia gave the Soviet Union one billion dollars of aid, which directly after the end of the Cold War was great for the Soviet Union not only because the money was tremendously helpful but also because it allowed the Soviets to ameliorate relations with the U.S.

On the other hand, Yemen was one of two countries that voted against this policy that essentially greenlighted further U.S. intervention into the Middle East, and in response, the United States ceased 70 million dollars worth of aid programs to Yemen. While since the 1990's the influence of the United States may have decreased or been challenged by other countries such as China, they remain the country with the most power and influence over the Security Council's actions.

When it comes to reforms of the Security Council, the United States has generally stayed much quieter than other permanent member countries. In terms of the veto, the United States has essentially not advocated for major veto reform because they frequently use the veto as a tool of foreign policy. This is especially the case when it comes to the controversy over Israel and Palestine, where the United States is a very close ally of Israel and has vetoed twelve separate resolutions surrounding Israel and Palestine since 2001.

In terms of expanding the Security Council, the United States has generally been open to the idea of adding new members, but only members that are allied with the U.S. and share similar ideas. For example, during the early years of Barack Obama's presidency, the United States said they were open to adding India as a permanent member of the council.

The reforms supported by the United States are not quite as substantive as the Security Council needs, and mainly serve to increase U.S. influence over the Security Council instead of fixing the structural issues the Security Council faces. Because of this, it is unlikely that these reforms will be sufficient to resolve issues with the Security Council, as just adding more U.S. allies as permanent members would do little more than making the Security Council more inefficient.

The People's Republic of China

Currently, the People's Republic of China is one of the five permanent members of the United Nations Security Councils. The East Asian country has had an extremely controversial history in the intergovernmental organization - most notably being its use of the Belt and Road Initiative to leverage a voting block made up of developing countries. President Xi Jinping has been known to strongarm other countries so he can control the general assembly, while simultaneously vetoing any resolution in the UNSC that is not favorable to China.

However, China's position on the UNSC hasn't always been one of dominance; in fact, it was quite the contrary. Let's take a deep dive into China's history on the UNSC, its agenda, and what it has in store for the future.

China joined the UN right when it was founded in 1945. However, the People's Republic of China went by a slightly different name in the beginning: The Republic of China. However, after the Chinese Civil War in the late 1940s, the People's Republic, led by the Chinese Communist Party, took over the country.

Importantly, most western countries opposed the replacement of the ROC with the PRC (led by

Chairman Mao), despite the fact that the ROC was operating in Taiwan. Eventually, in the 1970s, the global community recognized the PRC. On October 25th, 1971, after negotiations between Mao and President Nixon, an Albanian-proposed motion to recognize the PRC as the true and only representative of China to the UN passed. From that moment, the PRC has been a member of the United Nations and the United Nations Security Council.

The Republic of China only ever used its Security Council veto once, and it was to halt the admission of Mongolia into the United Nations in 1955. The ROC delegation argued that Mongolia was a part of China, and thus cannot have its own recognized delegation. In 1961, however, Mongolia was admitted to the United Nations. Additionally, the

ROC was one of the founding members of the United Nations Relief and Rehabilitation (UNRRA), which provided aid to countries under Axis (Nazi Germany, Imperial Japan, Fascist Italy) control. The UNRRA's biggest program was actually to China itself, which was under the control of Japan during World War Two, transferring over $600 million of foreign aid to China.

Once the People's Republic of China was recognized as the sole delegation for China at the United Nations, China's role, dominance, and influence in the organization exponentially grew. Simultaneously, the country's role became much more controversial. The PRC has used its veto power eight times, which even though is very impactful, is relatively far less than countries like Russia, which has used it 109 times. Most of the PRC's vetoes have been due to their One-China policy, which is essentially the belief that China and Taiwan are the same country and should be treated as such. For example, the PRC voted against a resolution that put ceasefire observers in Guatemala in 1997 because it recognized the ROC as the legitimate representative.

These uses of vetoes by the PRC have strongarmed the international community into not recognizing the Republic of China as a legitimate state. Additionally, much of the PRC's vetoes have been done in conjunction with Russia. Most notably, the PRC and Russia both vetoed sanctions against Syria and military intervention in Syria. Most foreign political analysts believe that this is due to the PRC's Belt and Road Initiative and its desire to curb US influence in the Middle East (Bashar Al-Assad, the President of Syria, is staunchly anti-US and pro-Russia). Analyst Giorgio Cafiero puts it best, saying that "two main objectives have driven China's Syria policies. First, in terms of security threats, Beijing wants to build a strong partnership with Damascus to maintain friendly ties and cooperate on counter-terrorism issues. Second, economically, the Chinese leadership seeks a Sino-Syrian relationship that helps Beijing advance its vision for the ambitious Belt and Road Initiative." Sadly, the PRC's forced UN inaction in Syria has led to thousands of civilian deaths at the hands of Assad.

Finally, the PRC's main impact on the UN and the UN Security Council is the Belt and Road Initiative. The Belt and Road Initiative is China's economic infrastructure plan to invest in 70 countries. Essentially, the PRC wants to better relations with countries in Africa, Asia, and Northern and Eastern Europe by investing in their economies, eventually culminating in the PRC having leverage over those countries. This can be seen prominently throughout Africa. The PRC has been engaging in "debt-trap diplomacy," using debt leverage through the BRI to pressure African countries to vote with China in the UN General Assembly. Rayna Martinez from the University of Nevada at Las Vegas said that "the sheer number of African states can dominate and influence voting outcomes of relevant issues in international affairs. With this in mind, China has emphasized and nurtured its relations with African member states of international organizations such as the UNGA, WTO, and the International Olympics Committee. In addition, African support through voting alignments enhances the PRC's domestic and international legitimacy." Rayna Martinez further qualifies the importance of these actions for the PRC: "Without the African voting bloc, China would not have been successful at transferring the UNSC seat from Taiwan to China. At present, only 4 African countries have diplomatic relations with Taiwan."

When it comes to reform of the United Nations Security Council, China has been notoriously against both veto reform and what would otherwise be the most popular suggested reform: the addition of India as a permanent member. This is largely due to the history of geopolitical tension and conflict between the two countries, which has caused China to repeatedly block attempts by the Security Council to add India. The only reform that China currently supports is the addition of more African nations to the Security Council as non-permanent members. While in the abstract this seems like a good idea, in reality the only African countries that China has proposed adding are those that they have substantial leverage over, meaning these changes would mostly further China's own foreign policy objectives while denying actual representation that would be beneficial for the majority of African countries. Additionally, China only supports the addition of these countries as non-permanent members and is opposed to expanding the list of permanent countries in any way, meaning China's proposed reforms would not even ensure lasting power for countries in

Africa. While China is certainly not the only reason reform is not happening, in a world where China did not have so much power India almost certainly would have become a permanent member of the Security Council by now.

The Russian Federation

The Soviet Union was actively attempting to expand its influence and political power in the 1940s, and the creation of the United Nations, as well as the United Nations Security Council, provided an ideal opportunity. Many of the structural issues of the security council can be attributed to the Soviet Union's attempts to limit the powers of other countries within the council. This can be seen most clearly through the creation of the veto, which the Soviet Union insisted was a crucial part of ensuring that the United Nations Security Council functioned properly. The Soviet Union argued that without the ability to veto, smaller countries would have too much power over the security council and would prevent the larger world powers from being able to properly ensure global security.

After the council was established and the USSR had a seat as a permanent member country, they proceeded to abuse the veto power to prevent the council from intervening in their foreign policy. Between the founding of the council and 1973, over 85 percent of vetoes were cast by the Soviet Union Ultimately, due to the United States and the Soviet Union both having a vested interest in the vast majority of global conflicts and also both having the ability to veto all substantive actions from the security council, during the cold war the security council rarely got involved in any major conflicts and instead played a limited role in mediating the disputes of smaller countries where neither the United States nor the Soviet Union had anything to gain.

After the fall of the Soviet Union and the formation of the Russian Federation, Russia was recognized as its legal descendant and became a permanent member in the Soviet Union's place. The United Nations Security Council was able to drastically expand the scope of its operations following the end of the cold war, and Russia has not played nearly as large of an inhibitory role as the Soviet Union once did. However, Russia has continued to use its power on the United Nations Security Council to primarily advance its own interests instead of the interests of the international community.

For example, Russia has repeatedly taken actions on the security council attempting to deny the sovereignty of states that used to be part of the Soviet Union like Moldova and Ukraine, including blocking security council action concerning Crimea. In spite of using vetoes far less than the Soviet Union, Russia has also continued to use its vetoes to advance its own foreign policy and protect its allies. Russia has continuously advocated on behalf of Syria's corrupt and oppressive government, vetoing multiple resolutions that would investigate or condemn Syria's potential uses of chemical weapons against its civilians and then vetoing a resolution that would have increased international aid to Syrian civilians.

Due to some recent calls to reform the United Nations Security Council and some calls to almost entirely overhaul it, Russia has surprisingly been in favor of many initiatives to change the council. However, under further inspection, it becomes clear that any changes Russia is in favor of are those that allow them to keep the veto power, retain a dominant position on the council, and only give more representation to countries that they have political ties to. Russia benefits greatly from the status quo, so it makes sense that they want to retain it. Russia views the United Nations Security Council as a hegemonic intergovernmental organization that needs to have the final say in security disputes around the world, which is why they are in favor of moderate reform but nothing that fundamentally changes the council.

Russia sees calls for change as threats to the institutional capital of the security council and sees reforms as something to appease those who want change without actually delivering substantive change. Ultimately, any major reform to the United Nations Security Council looks unlikely if Russia continues to prioritize its own allies and foreign policy objectives over the global security that the council was made to protect.

The United Kingdom

The United Kingdom is a founding member of the UN Security Council, and thus has a permanent seat on the Security Council. However, the biggest impact the UK has had on the security council came during the UNSC's infancy. During the famous Yalta Conference, where the structure of the UNSC was decided upon, Winston Churchill urged that France be included as a permanent member of the Security Council, despite not being a part of the Four Powers. The Four Powers, the US, UK, Soviet Union, and China, were considered the main Allied forces in World War 2, and thus were the easy choices as permanent members of the security council. Despite this, Churchill wanted to revitalize France's reputation as a major power, which it had before World War 2 and secured its spot on the council. Without the efforts of Churchill and by proxy the United Kingdom, France would have likely been left off the UN Security Council, and the role of the UNSC could be much different than what we see today.

Despite the power, the UK holds with their veto, for the past 30 years they've been relatively inactive. The UK has the third most vetoes in UNSC history, behind the Soviet Union/Russia and the US, but they haven't vetoed a single resolution since the end of the cold war. Furthermore, the only issue they've been the lone vetoing power on is that of

Southern Rhodesia. The only other member that has been the lone vetoing power less than the UK is France. The reason the UK was willing to veto action on Southern Rhodesia is because Southern Rhodesia was effectively a British colony after 1923, and during the period of their vetoes was the Rhodesian Bush War, which was a 15-year conflict that eventually resulted in the renaming to Zimbabwe-Rhodesia and a power-sharing agreement between white and black people in the country. The UK's Prime Minister Margaret Thatcher refused to recognize the internal settlement, which was the agreement within Zimbabwe-Rhodesia that created this power-sharing agreement, as legitimate. Before the renaming and internal settlement, however, there was evidence of chemical weapons in the conflict used against Black

Nationalists, and numerous countries in Africa requested that the UN Security Council officially investigated the situation in Rhodesia. The UK would veto this request a total of seven times, five of which they were the only vetoing member. The UK's repeated veto of this request is the biggest example of its use of its seat on the UNSC to further its own agenda.

Another key role the UK has played throughout the Security Council's history is as a key ally to the US. Being the only member to veto a resolution looks optically terrible for any member, but having two members veto looks much better. This has been the story of the US and the UK. They have vetoed together on 22 different occasions, famously including the resolution to condemn the US invasion of Panama. This meant the US' excuse of self-defense, which does not apply to an invasion, was supported by the US, UK, and France who also vetoed the resolution. Although the resolution to condemn the US was clearly justified, the optics of three member states vetoing is what is important to this discussion. The United Nations Security Council has long been a place for member states to either exert their power or control the narrative around their actions, and that is exactly what the UK has helped the US do. By vetoing with the US, the UK makes this invasion seem legitimate, unlike the violation of international law that it is.

In more recent times, the UK has been very passive with its role in the UNSC. The only sources of controversy have been its lack of action, most recently with Myanmar. There have been numerous calls for action from the UNSC on the military control of Myanmar, but the UK has done nothing. Although it isn't just their fault, they have done nothing of substance other than verbally condemning the events in Myanmar. Many countries but especially the UK have prioritized having the UNSC speak as one uniform voice instead of actually trying to get resolutions passed that would foster change. This a continuation of the theme where the UK will value optics more than substantial action, something also very prominent in their allyship with the US.

Overall, the UK had its most influence at the beginning of the UNSC, and similar to every other member they have used their power to further their own agenda, especially with their former colonies. Despite this controversial history, the UK still has the opportunity to change that narrative with actions on current and future issues. Action on the military in Myanmar, the subjugation of Uyghur Muslims in China, and numerous other conflicts around the world could prove that the UK's claims about their commitment to peace are more than just empty rhetoric.

In terms of reform to the Security Council, the UK has been in favor of reform for far longer than most other countries and is in favor of more expansive reform than most permanent members. It supports the expansion of both permanent and non-permanent members seats from the current fifteen to an unspecified number in the high to mid-twenties. However, while they have mentioned methods of countries working together outside of the Security Council after a veto, they have not been a supporter of substantive reform to the veto power. While the UK is not the reason reform is not happening in the status quo, it also has not favored reforms that would directly reduce its power. Ultimately the UK is more progressive when it comes to reform than most permanent members but still falls short of suggesting reforms that would change the fundamental power structure of the United Nations Security Council.

The French Republic

In the year 2021, seeing France as one of the five permanent members of the United Nations Security Council might seem strange. Not only is Europe already represented in contrast with regions like the Middle East, Africa, and South America, but France has far less of a proclivity for intervention in global affairs. To properly understand France's role on the council it is important to first understand why they were included as a permanent member in the first place. While France played a fairly large role in the Second World War, it was ultimately their geographical location that got them a permanent seat on the Security Council.

The United States and the United Kingdom both wanted a continental European country on the Security Council in order to better police Europe, as following both world wars Europe seemed to be the largest potential hotspot for conflict that would require the Security Council's intervention. Germany and Italy were not going to be chosen for fairly obvious reasons, so France was picked as the next most influential country in continental Europe mainly due to Winston Churchill's insistence that France was necessary for the Security Council to actually be effective.

Ever since its inclusion, France has used its veto incredibly sparingly, instead opting to be more of a neutral member of the Security Council that largely tries to actually protect international security. In fact, France has used the veto less than any other permanent member country, something that China used to be able to claim before the past few decades where they have used the veto frequently. However, France has still abused the veto power on several occasions in order to further their own interests instead of those of the international community. The most important example of this comes in the form of France's vetoes of resolutions surrounding Mayotte. Without getting too much into the complex and messy history of French colonization, both France and the Union of the Comoros believe that the island of

Mayotte should be considered their territory. In the 1970s, resolutions that would have the United Nations Security Council intervene and determine who should rightfully control Mayotte were vetoed by the French government. This is a great example of political theater in the Security Council, as everyone who pushed forward these resolutions knew they were going to be vetoed by France, but also knew France would be looked down upon by members of the international community by using the veto for selfish purposes.

France has since taken a far more progressive view on the Security Council, being the permanent member who has been most in favor of substantive reform. Concerning the veto, France has not used their veto power since 1989 and is in favor of reforming what situations the veto can be used in. This comes primarily in the form of the French Initiative, which would not allow the veto to be used in cases of mass atrocity.

France has also taken a progressive stance in terms of expanding the Security Council, as they are in favor of adding Germany, India, Brazil, and Japan as permanent member countries. A shift from five to nine permanent members would greatly change the balance of the Security Council, but it is worth noting that some veto reform would be necessary if such a change was to occur. Finally, unlike other countries, France has actually taken action that seems to indicate that they truly believe in reform, unlike every other permanent member who continues to simultaneously claim they are fine with reform while also abusing their power and blocking change from taking place. France took a historic step in 2019 when they shared their term as president of the Security Council with Germany. This act, while largely symbolic, allowed France and Germany to both have equal power of the presidency leading to increased cooperation and trust between the two European nations. It is clear that while France has a problematic past with the Security Council, nowadays they are the permanent member most open to change and least tolerant to abuse.

Non-Permanent Members

Throughout the history of the United Nations Security Council, hundreds of different countries have served as non-permanent members. While it is clear that these temporary members of the council do not have nearly as much power or influence as the permanent members, it is still interesting to study what they have been able to do with their limited power and, perhaps more importantly, what they have been unable to do. While it would be impractical to study every single non-permanent member, this chapter will go over two of the most important and influential examples.

Malaysia

Malaysia is a country that has been on the Security Council several times and despite being a non-permanent member has had a number of meaningful and consequential actions. Like many non-permanent members, Malaysia does not have the ability to resolve many issues on its own because it does not have the military or economic influence some countries hold. This has caused Malaysia to view the Security Council as being extremely important and has historically tried to use it as a means of reaching justice.

This can be seen most clearly after Malaysia Airlines flight MH17, which was shot down in a part of Ukraine that was controlled by Russia. This not only was tragic for many Malaysian citizens, it also had long lasting effects on travel to Malaysia and to international perception of Malaysia's security, as well as setting an extremely problematic precedent for use of military force against civilian aircraft. Malaysia attempted to create an international tribunal to prosecute those involved in destroying the plane, but this ultimately failed as Russia used its veto power to stop the tribunal from being made. This example illustrates the issue with the Security Council, it is the main avenue for countries with smaller economies and militaries to resolve disputes, but the large countries that already have geopolitical power outside of the council are the ones with the most power on the council. However, Malaysia has still managed to make an impact despite its lack of power. United Nations Security Council Resolution 2334 was sponsored by Malaysia and set an important precedent that as far as international law is concerned, Israel had made settlements in Palestinian territory that had no legal basis. This also led to the Security Council demanding Israel stopped encroachment on Palestinian territory as they were causing conflict. While Malaysia was the sponsor of this resolution, it is only because no permanent member was opposed to the resolution that it was able to pass.

Venezuela

Venezuela has not been on the council in years, and as much of the international community views the current state of politics too unstable it is unlikely they will get a seat any time soon. Over the past couple of years, Venezuela has written several letters to the United Nations Security Council concerning border disputes between Colombia and Venezuela as well as the deployment of United States ships near Venezuela's coast. Despite both issues at the border and on the coast harming Venezuela's economy and travel to Venezuela, these letters have largely had no effect on the Security Council's proceedings.

During the height of political instability and protests after Nicolás Maduro's second inauguration, the United States drafted a resolution that attempted to intervene in order to attempt to institute a fair democracy. This was vetoed by both Russia and China, one of the rare instances where multiple permanent members veto the same resolution.

Despite all this, Venezuela has had a significant impact on the historical development of the Security Council through Arria-Formula meetings. These meetings, named after Venezuelan diplomat Diego Arria, can be called by any member instead of traditional meetings that can only be called by the president. These essentially serve as informal meetings where different countries on the Security

Council can communicate confidentially without the bureaucratic restraints of a typical meeting. Ever since the Security Council started having Arria-Formula meetings it has been much more efficient, because countries can now get a better sense of where each other stand much faster. While the Security Council might currently be ignoring Venezuela, Venezuela was extremely important to the development of the Security Council's procedures without having the power of a permanent member country.

The Importance of Non-Permanent Members

Ultimately, almost every non-permanent member country has caused some important development in the Security Council's history even with the minimal influence afforded to them by the structures of the Security Council. Because many of these countries are much smaller and less involved in global affairs, they generally have the interests of the international community in mind more than it seems most permanent members do. Instead of trying to abuse their power to protect their allies, smaller countries generally use their power to set precedents that are crucial for ensuring the Security Council protects all territories regardless of size. In most of the literature regarding changing the United Nation's Security Council, non-permanent member countries are rarely discussed as a major factor, but due to their importance in the Security Council's history, it is important that any changes that occur take into account the role that non-permanent members will be able to play in a reformed United Nations Security Council.

Conclusion

The United Nations Security Council needs reform. It has the potential to enact peace and ensure the powers of the world work together, but for its whole history, it acted as a means for 5 countries to exert their influence on the rest of the world and ensure smaller countries' don't have any ways to force the UN's hand in conflicts the 5 powers might have a vested interest in. The veto power the 5 nations have is arguably the most powerful act any country can have on a diplomatic scale, and it needs to change.

The veto is almost always used to prevent helpful resolutions from being passed because they would negatively affect a few of the permanent members. It is arbitrary and no longer serves a purpose in regulating other countries. The original purpose of the veto was to ensure that groups of smaller countries couldn't unjustifiably exert their power on the rest of the UN, but now it just means no amount of non-permanent members is enough unless all 5 permanent members are on board for a resolution, which they almost never are.

In order to reform the veto, there have many different ideas as to what would work. Some say that restricting the veto only to "vital national security issues" would work, but this is incredibly vague, and situations like the US claiming that the invasion of Panama was an act of self-defense might still apply. Although a more specific version of this revision to the veto system might be successful, as of right now such reforms don't exist. Another possible revision would be to force two vetoes instead of just one for a resolution to be rejected. This in theory would prevent cases like the blocking of the investigation of Panama and Rhodesia, and also countless of the Soviet Union's vetoes. The issue with this proposal is that in almost every case that there is a single country vetoing, they have an ally who would vote with them if it came to that. This means there would be very few instances where only one permanent member was using their veto power, and a similar amount of resolutions would be rejected. Furthermore, the optics of two vetoing powers versus one vetoing power means a country would never solely be at fault for a resolution getting rejected, and just say they were following their ally. This would further skirt culpability from member countries, which would be counterproductive to the reform's goal.

Arguably the most effective and most radical reform would be to abolish the veto power altogether. If the veto power was completely abolished, then there would be no exceptions that countries could exploit to continue the veto like the other reforms. This would mean the Security Council's founders' biggest fear would come true, the majority of smaller countries could override the desires of the permanent members. The difference now is that we know the Security Council never acts with the world's best interests at heart, but instead just their own. This means in the future, the desires of a majority of smaller countries would likely lead to more resolutions being passed, more investigations into human rights violations, and ideally would force countries to consider the international ramifications of their actions. The main thing stopping any of these reforms from happening is that for these reforms to be passed, they would have to be voted on, and any of the five permanent members could veto the reform to the veto. Clearly, it is improbable that any permanent member, much less all five, would allow a reform like these to pass.

Other than reforms to the veto, there are also possibilities of new permanent members. Any new permanent member could drastically change how the UNSC functions, especially if they are not strongly affiliated with an existing permanent member. The most controversy has been surrounding India's possible induction. India was made a non-permanent member in January of 2021, but its ultimate goal is to gain a permanent seat. This of course would grant them all the powers that the existing permanent members have, most importantly the veto. Thus, they have set out to become an integral part of the UNSC during their temporary membership, so they will have a very good case of becoming a permanent member when their current stint ends at the beginning of 2023. Their permanent seat could be a result of their continued importance to the UN's peacekeeping missions and overall their contribution via their military. The issue is, there have been countries in the past that have had a similar level of participation as India, and they were never added to the UNSC permanently. The other major reason for

India's inclusion would be that they are the biggest democracy in the world, yet are not a permanent member of a council that includes countries far smaller than it. Despite their existing justifications for inclusion, India needs to do something major to make their case stronger for being added, and they need to do it soon.

There are three other countries that are vying for a permanent seat, those being Brazil, Germany, and Japan. Unlike India, none of these countries have much of an argument past their economic contributions. The only country close to India's bid for candidacy is Japan, and this is mainly because Japan and India have linked their bid for candidacies. India and Japan are both members of the G4, and thus strongly support each other's candidacy. This has actually hurt India's bid for candidacy, as China has stated they would support India's candidacy if they weren't so closely linked with Japan. Conversely, this has helped Japan's candidacy, making them look like they have as much influence as India when in reality they have contributed much less to the UN.

Overall, it's clear the UN Security Council needs to change. Whether that comes in the form of a reform to the veto system or adding a new permanent member to balance some of the power, it would be better than nothing. Without reforms, it will continue on its current trajectory of promoting individual interests and doing nothing to stop permanent members from furthering their own harmful agendas.

References

1. • Alexander, Titus (1996). Unravelling Global Apartheid: An Overview of World Politics. Cambridge, Massachusetts: Polity Press. ISBN 978-0-7456-1353-6.

2. • Alghadawi, Abdullah, et al. "China Plays the Long Game on Syria." Middle East Institute, 24 Sept. 2021, https://www.mei.edu/publications/china-plays-long-game-syria.

3. • Bailey, Sydney D.; Daws, Sam (1998). The Procedure of the UN Security Council (3rd ed.). Oxford University Press. ISBN 978-0-19-828073-6.

4. • Blum, Yehuda Z. (1992). "Russia Takes Over the Soviet Union's Seat at the United Nations"(PDF).

European Journal of International Law. 3 (2): 354–362. doi:10.1093/ejil/3.2.354.

5. • Bosco, David L. (2009). Five to Rule Them All: The UN Security Council and the Making of the Modern World. New York: Oxford University Press. ISBN 978-0-19-532876-9.

6. • Cockayne, James; Mikulaschek, Christoph; Perry, Chris (2010). The United Nations Security Council and Civil War: First Insights from a New Dataset. New York: International Peace Institute.

7. • Coulon, Jocelyn (1998). Soldiers of Diplomacy: The United Nations, Peacekeeping, and the New World Order. University of Toronto Press. ISBN 978-0-8020-0899-2.

8. • Deni, John R. (2007). Alliance Management and Maintenance: Restructuring NATO for the 21st

Century. Aldershot, England: Ashgate Publishing. ISBN 978-0-7546-7039-1.

9. • Fasulo, Linda (2004). An Insider's Guide to the UN. New Haven, Connecticut: Yale University Press. ISBN 978-0-300-10155-3.

10. • Fomerand, Jacques (2009). The A to Z of the United Nations. Lanham, Maryland: Scarecrow Press. ISBN 978-0-8108-5547-2.

11. • Gaddis, John Lewis (2000) [1972]. The United States and the Origins of the Cold War, 1941–1947. New York: Columbia University Press. ISBN 978-0-231-12239-9.

12. • Grieger, Gisela (2013). Reform of the UN Security Council (PDF). Library of the European Parliament.

13. • Hannay, David (2008). New World Disorder: The UN after the Cold War – An Insider's View. London: I.B. Tauris. ISBN 978-1-84511-719-1.

14. • Hillier, Timothy (1998). Sourcebook on Public International Law. Sourcebook Series. London: Cavendish Publishing. ISBN 978-1-85941-050-9.

15. • Hoopes, Townsend; Brinkley, Douglas (2000) [1997]. FDR and the Creation of the U.N. New Haven, Connecticut: Yale University Press. ISBN 978-0-300-08553-2.

16. • Hurd, Ian (2007). After Anarchy: Legitimacy and Power in the United Nations Security Council. Princeton, New Jersey: Princeton University Press. ISBN 978-0-691-12866-5.

17. • Kennedy, Paul (2006). The Parliament of Man: The Past, Present, and Future of the United Nations. New York: Random House. ISBN 978-0-375-50165-4.

18. • Köchler, Hans (2001). The Concept of Humanitarian Intervention in the Context of Modern Power: Is the Revival of the Doctrine of "Just War" Compatible with the International Rule of Law?. Studies in International Relations. 26. Vienna: International Progress Organization. ISBN 978-3-900704-20-9.

19. • Köchler, Hans (1991). The Voting Procedure in the United Nations Security Council: Examining a Normative Contradiction in the UN Charter and its Consequences on International Relations (PDF). Studies in International Relations. 17. Vienna:

International Progress Organization. ISBN 978-3-900704-10-0.

20. • Lowe, Vaughan; Roberts, Adam; Welsh, Jennifer; Zaum, Dominik, eds. (2008). The United Nations Security Council and War: The Evolution of Thought and Practice since 1945. Oxford University Press. ISBN 978-0-19-953343-5.

21. • Magliveras, Konstantinos D. (1999). Exclusion from Participation in International Organisations: The Law and Practice behind Member States' Expulsion and Suspension of Membership. Studies and Materials on the Settlement of International Disputes. 5. The Hague: Kluwer Law International. ISBN 978-90-411-1239-2.

22. • Malone, David (1998). Decision-Making in the UN Security Council: The Case of Haiti, 1990–1997. Oxford: Clarendon Press. ISBN 978-0-19-829483-2.

23. • Manchester, William; Reid, Paul (2012). The Last Lion: Winston Spencer Churchill. Volume 3: Defender of the Realm. New York: Little Brown and Company. ISBN 978-0-316-54770-3.

24. • Martinez, Rayna, "Chinese Soft power, Africa, and the United Nations General Assembly" (2015). UNLV Theses, Dissertations, Professional Papers, and Capstones. 2490. https://digitalscholarship.unlv.edu/thesesdissertations/2490

25. • Matheson, Michael J. (2006). Council Unbound: The Growth of UN Decision Making on Conflict and

Postconflict Issues after the Cold War. Washington: US Institute of Peace Press. ISBN 978-1-929223-78-7.

26. • Matthews, Ken (1993). The Gulf Conflict and International Relations. London: Routledge. ISBN 978-0-415-07519-0.

27. • Meisler, Stanley (1995). United Nations: The First Fifty Years. New York: Atlantic Monthly Press.

28. • Mikulaschek, Christoph (2010). "Report from the 39th International Peace Institute Vienna Seminar on Peacemaking and Peacekeeping". In Winkler, Hans; Rød-Larsen, Terje; Mikulaschek, Christoph (eds.). The UN Security Council and the Responsibility to Protect: Policy, Process, and Practice (PDF). Favorita Papers. Diplomatic Academy of Vienna. pp. 20–49. ISBN 978-3-902021-67-0.

29. • Mires, Charlene (2013). Capital of the World: The Race to Host the United Nations. New York University Press. ISBN 978-0-8147-0794-4.

30. • Neuhold, Hanspeter (2001). "The United Nations System for the Peaceful Settlement of International Disputes". In Cede, Frank; Sucharipa-Behrmann, Lilly (eds.). The United Nations: Law and Practice. The Hague: Kluwer Law International. ISBN 978-90-411-1563-8.

31. • Osmańczyk, Edmund Jan (2004). Mango, Anthony (ed.). Encyclopedia of the United Nations and International Agreements. 4. Taylor & Francis. ISBN 978-0-415-93924-9.

32. • Roberts, Adam; Zaum, Dominik (2008). Selective Security: War and the United Nations Security Council since 1945. Strategic Survey : The

Annual Review of World Affairs. Adelphi Paper. 395. Abingdon, England: Routledge. ISBN 978-0-415-47472-6.

33. • Schlesinger, Stephen C. (2003). Act of Creation: The Founding of the United Nations: A Story of Super Powers, Secret Agents, Wartime Allies and Enemies, and Their Quest for a Peaceful World. Boulder, Colorado: Westview Press. ISBN 978-0-8133-3324-3.

34. • Vreeland, James; Dreher, Axel (2014). The Political Economy of the United Nations Security Council: Money and Influence. Cambridge, England: Cambridge University Press. ISBN 978-0-521-51841-3.

35. • Wilcox, Francis O. (1945). "The Yalta Voting Formula". American Political Science Review. 39(5): 943–956. doi:10.2307/1950035.

36. • Zunes, Stephen (2004). "International Law, the UN and Middle Eastern Conflicts". Peace Review: A Journal of Social Justice. 16 (3): 285–292. doi:10.1080/1040265042000278513

37. Bardo Fassbender, 'Pressure for Security Council Reform', in: David M. Malone (ed.), The UN Security Council: From the Cold War to the 21st Century, Lynne Rienner Publishers, Boulder, Colorado, and London, 2004, pp. 341–355.

38. Bardo Fassbender, 'The Security Council: Progress is Possible but Unlikely', in: Antonio Cassese (ed.), Realizing Utopia: The Future of International Law, Oxford University Press, 2012, pp. 52–60.

39. Bardo Fassbender, UN Security Council Reform and the Right of Veto: A Constitutional Perspective,

Kluwer Law International, The Hague / London / Boston, 1998. ISBN 90-411-0592-1.

40. David Malone (ed), The UN Security Council: From the Cold War to the 21st Century, Lynne Rienner, Boulder, Colorado, 2004. ISBN 1-58826-240-5

41. Vaughan Lowe; Adam Roberts; Jennifer Welsh; Dominik Zaum (eds.). The United Nations Security Council and War: The Evolution of Thought and Practice since 1945, Oxford University Press, 2008. ISBN 978-0-19-953343-5

Printed in Great Britain
by Amazon